ANIMAL ALBUMS

THE FISH FAMILY

BY ALEX MONROE

Eureka!

EUREKA!, AN IMPRINT OF BELLWETHER MEDIA BY FLUTTERBEE

Eureka! books turn real stories into unforgettable experiences. Clear, direct language and sharp, captivating imagery make it easy to follow your curiosity, one fascinating fact at a time.
Your Eureka! moment awaits!

This edition first published in 2027 by Bellwether Media, Inc.

Names: Monroe, Alex author
Title: The fish family / By Alex Monroe.
Description: Eureka. | Minneapolis, MN : Bellwether Media, Inc, 2027. | Series: Animal albums | Includes index. | Audience: Ages 9-13 | Audience: Grades 7-9 | Summary: "Engaging images accompany information on fish. The text level and subject matter are intended for students in grades 5 through 9"-- Provided by publisher.
Identifiers: LCCN 2026010706 (print) | LCCN 2026010707 (ebook) | ISBN 9798898801304 (library binding) | ISBN 9798898802547 (ebook)
Subjects: LCSH: Fishes--Juvenile literature | LCGFT: Juvenile literature
Classification: LCC QL617.2 .M65 2027 (print) | LCC QL617.2 (ebook) | DDC 597--dc23/eng/20260220
LC record available at https://lccn.loc.gov/2026010706
LC ebook record available at https://lccn.loc.gov/2026010707

Editor: Nathan Sommer Series Designer: Jeff Kollock

Printed in the United States of America, North Mankato, MN.

TABLE OF CONTENTS

WHAT ARE FISH? 4

THE HISTORY OF FISH 6

LIFE CYCLE 8

FISH LANGUAGE AND BEHAVIOR 10

FISH FAMILY TREE 12

FISH BIOGRAPHIES 14

FISH AND PEOPLE 42

GLOSSARY 46

WRITE ABOUT IT! 47

INDEX 48

WHAT ARE FISH?

There are more than 30,000 fish species. They live in most marine and freshwater habitats. Some fish are jawless. Others have cartilage instead of bones. Many are bony fish.

MARLIN

▲ PEACOCK FLOUNDERS

◀ WEEDY SEA DRAGON

▲ BETTA FISH

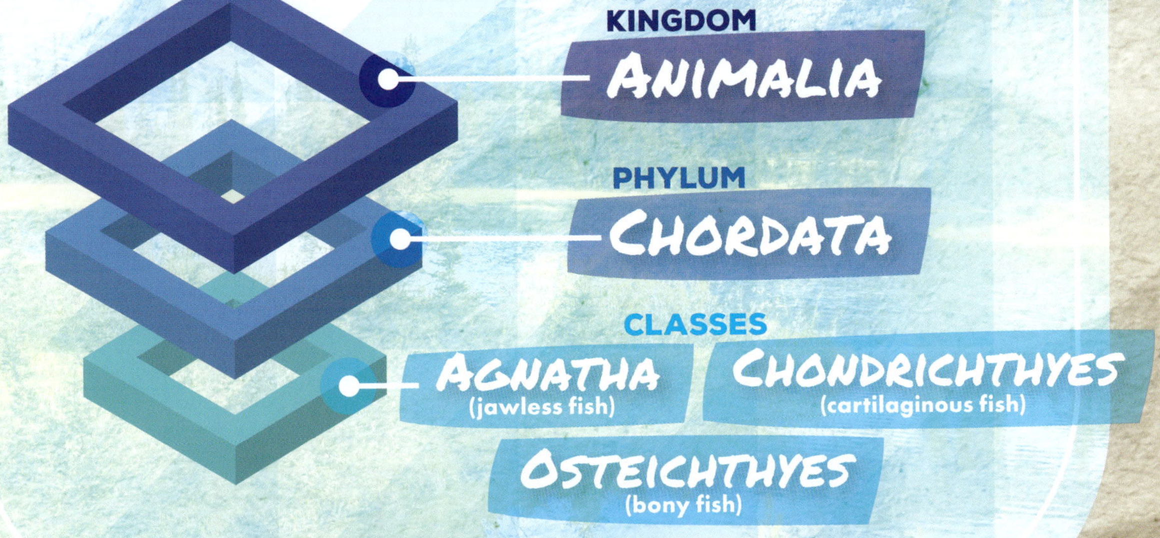

TAXONOMY CHART

Fish make up a hugely diverse group of animals. The many species are very different from one another. But most fish share several qualities and behaviors. All fish are vertebrates. They have paired fins. Most fish have gills that allow them to breathe underwater. A majority are cold-blooded. Many species have scales.

▼ FLOWERHORN CICHLID

KOI FISH ▲
in a garden pond

LONGHORN ▲
COWFISH

THE HISTORY OF FISH

The earliest fish lived around 500 million years ago. These jawless fish were slow-swimming bottom dwellers. They were the first animals with backbones. Bony plates covered their bodies. Their fins were not fully formed.

Around 400 million years ago, many different types of fish evolved. The first fish with paired fins appeared, and early sharks developed. Some fish developed jaws as more animals evolved. The first bony fish developed.

A COMMON RELATIVE

Millions of years ago, some fish began crawling on land. They also formed lungs to breathe air. All animals with backbones evolved from these fish.

Fish have adapted to live in waters around the world. The great diversity in their bodies and behaviors has helped many species thrive.

EVOLUTIONARY EXCELLENCE

LIFE
CYCLE

Fish reproduce in different ways. A few species give birth to live babies. Most fish spawn. Females release eggs into the water. Then males fertilize the eggs. Many species leave their eggs after spawning. Some carefully watch over their eggs. There are species, such as some catfish, that carry eggs in their mouths.

SEAHORSE
live birth

CLOWNFISH EGGS

▲ **JAWFISH**
protecting eggs in its mouth

ANGELFISH ▶
laying eggs

SCALING UP

As fish get bigger, their scales do too. New rings form around the edges of their scales as they grow.

Larvae hatch and feed from their yolk sacs. They become fry once they have fully eaten their yolk sacs. Most fry are very small, but they grow quickly. Juvenile fish look like small adults. Their scales and fins develop. Fish become adults when they are ready to spawn.

▲ **DISCUS** parent with fry

HOW MANY YOUNG?

ATLANTIC HERRING

200,000 EGGS

BELUGA STURGEON

7,000,000 EGGS

GIANT MANTA RAY

1 PUP

CHINOOK SALMON

17,000 EGGS

FISH LANGUAGE AND BEHAVIOR

COMMUNICATION

Many fish make sounds, such as purrs, croaks, and pops, to breed or fight. Some fish talk by making grating sounds with their teeth. Fish may use body colors, patterns, and bioluminescence to communicate. Some fish give off chemicals.

LIONFISH ▲

▼ BIOLUMINESCENT ANGLERFISH

SCHOOLING

Some fish form groups called schools. These groups often stay together for life. Schools swim together in formation. The movements schools make often help fish avoid and confuse predators.

SCHOOL OF FISH ▶

MIGRATION

Many fish migrate to find food. Some travel daily from deep to shallow waters. Others are always on the move. They can migrate thousands of miles each year. Some species migrate to spawn.

KOKANEE SALMON▲
migrating upstream

FISH FAMILY
TREE

BONY FISH

Osteichthye

▲LUNGFISH

Lungfish can walk! Flexible shoulders allow these fish to use their fins to move along riverbeds.

▲STURGEONS

EELS▲

Moray eels have two sets of jaws. Their main jaws capture prey. Smaller jaws in their throats pull prey into their digestive tracts.

▲ANGLERFISH

Some species of anglerfish create light at the end of their spines. The light helps attract prey and mates.

▲SEAHORSES

Female seahorses put their eggs in males' stomach pouches. Males fertilize the eggs and carry them while the young develop. Then males give birth to live fry.

▲CATFISH

▲TUNA

PUFFER FISH▲

\+ MORE THAN **29,000** OTHER SPECIES

CHORDATA

CARTILAGINOUS FISH

Chondrichthyes

▲ RAYS

+ MORE THAN 1,000 OTHER SPECIES

JAWLESS FISH

Agnatha

LAMPREYS ▲

+ AROUND 110 OTHER SPECIES

LAMPREYS

Lampreys are jawless and boneless fish. There are more than 40 species.

PACIFIC LAMPREY
Range in the Wild

WHERE DO THEY LIVE?

Most lampreys live in temperate coastal waters of the Atlantic and Pacific Oceans. Some are also found in freshwater lakes and rivers near coasts.

DIET

Some lamprey species are parasites. They latch onto fish. Then they feed on blood. Other species do not feed as adults.

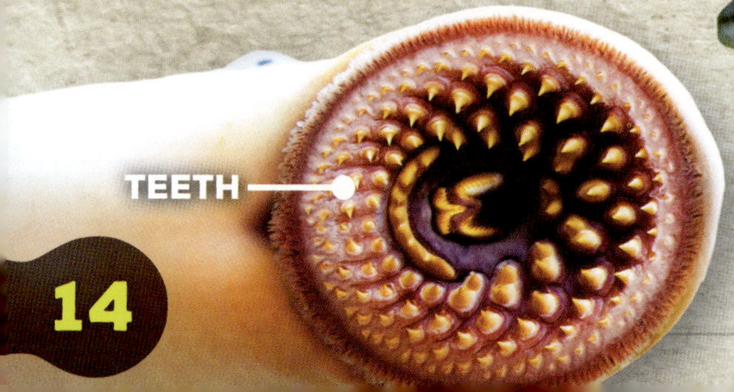

▲ **FISH** with lampreys attached

APPEARANCE

These fish have long bodies without scales. They can be light brown to blue-black in color. Countershading is common. They have one or two fins on their backs and a tail fin. Hornlike teeth fill their wide, round mouths.

SPECIES PROFILE

PACIFIC LAMPREY

- **Range:** Pacific coasts and coastal rivers of Asia and North America
- **Known for:** Pacific lampreys have existed for more than 450 million years. These fish make great migrations between freshwater rivers and ocean waters. They are important members of their ecosystems.

YOUNG LAMPREYS ▼

SIZE COMPARISON

2.5 FT (0.76 m)

Pacific lamprey

6 FT (1.8 m)

green moray eel

26 FT (8 m)

beluga sturgeon

RAYS

There are more than 630 ray species. They include different types of rays, sawfishes, and skates.

SAWFISH ▼

APPEARANCE

Rays have flat, wide bodies. They flap their large pectoral fins to swim. Many have long, whiplike tails. Some have venomous spines that stick out of their tails.

MANTA RAY

DIET

Rays often eat animals that live beneath the sand. This includes clams, crabs, and shrimp. Larger rays hunt squid and small fish. They often suck prey into their mouths.

STINGRAY ▲
feeding

GIANT MANTA RAY

Range in the Wild

WHERE DO THEY LIVE?

Rays swim in oceans worldwide. They are found in both open seas and coastal waters. Most live along the seafloor.

A WIDE WINGSPAN

The largest rays have wingspans of 26 feet (7.9 meters).

SIZE COMPARISON

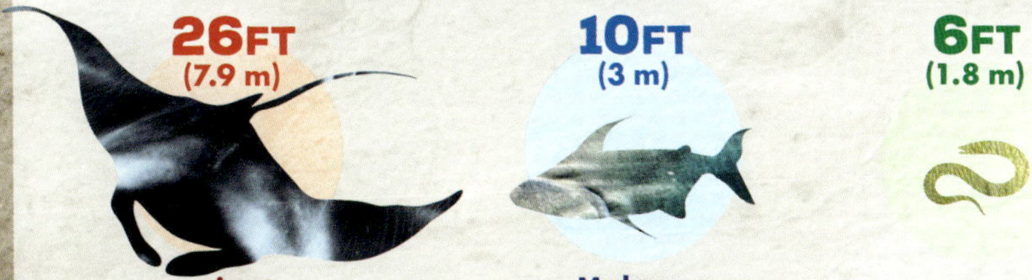

26FT (7.9 m)	10FT (3 m)	6FT (1.8 m)
giant manta ray	Mekong giant catfish	green moray eel

VULNERABLE SPECIES

GIANT MANTA RAY

▼ ENDANGERED ▼

THREATS

- bycatch
- overfishing

CONSERVATION EFFORTS ▼

- programs to reduce bycatch
- population monitoring
- community education

LUNGFISH

Lungfish must breathe air to survive. This helps many lungfish live in habitats that do not have water year-round.

APPEARANCE

Lungfish have long, slender bodies that are often spotted. Their backbones reach the ends of their finned tails. Some species have long, stringy pectoral fins.

DIET

Lungfish eat different aquatic animals. Some hunt members of their own species. These fish suck prey into their mouths, then crush it with their teeth. They may also eat roots and seeds.

▲ AUSTRALIAN LUNGFISH

SIZE COMPARISON

10FT (3 m)

Mekong giant catfish

7FT (2.1 m)

African marbled lungfish

6.6FT (2 m)

common monkfish

▼ SOUTH AMERICAN LUNGFISH

SPECIES PROFILE

AFRICAN MARBLED LUNGFISH

- **Range:** eastern and central Africa

- **Known for:** These fish are also called leopard lungfish. Dark spots along their bodies look like the coat of a leopard.

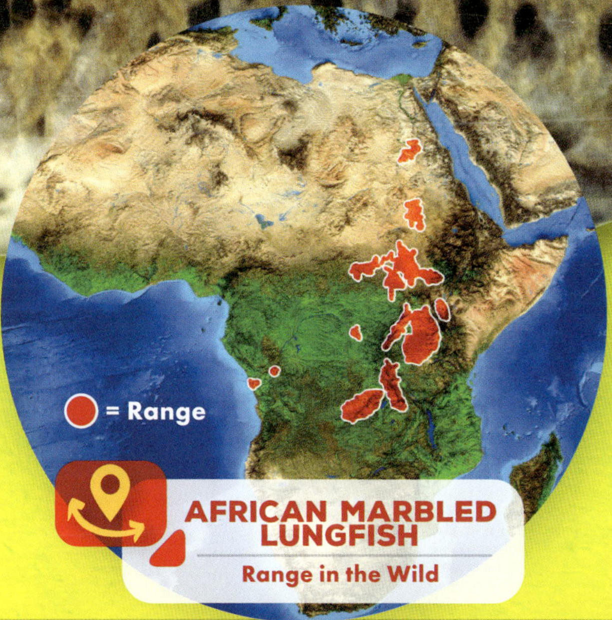

AFRICAN MARBLED LUNGFISH
Range in the Wild

WHERE DO THEY LIVE?

Lungfish live in and near tropical freshwater lakes and rivers. Four species live in Africa. One lives in South America, and one lives in Australia.

STURGEONS

Sturgeons are some of the largest freshwater fish. Some grow longer than 20 feet (6.1 meters). There are more than 20 species.

WHERE DO THEY LIVE?

Sturgeons are found throughout the northern hemisphere. Most live in the ocean but spawn in fresh water. Some only live in fresh water.

DIET

Sturgeons are bottom feeders. They use barbels to sense small fishes and invertebrates. Their tubelike mouths sit on the underside of their heads. When they sense prey, they suck in food and swallow it whole.

SPECIES PROFILE

Beluga Sturgeon

- **Range:**
  Caspian Sea, Black Sea, Sea of Azov

- **Known for:**
  Beluga sturgeons are the largest sturgeon species. They are also the fastest growing species. These fish can live to be over 100 years old!

APPEARANCE

Sturgeons have bony plates that cover their heads and form lines down their bodies. They have dark backs and light-colored bellies.

FANCY FOOD

Caviar is a luxury food made from fish eggs. It is often used as a spread. Several species of sturgeon eggs are commonly used for this fancy food.

SIZE COMPARISON

3FT (1 m)	7FT (2.1 m)	26FT (8 m)
Chinook salmon	African marbled lungfish	beluga sturgeon

EELS

Eels are fish that have long, snakelike bodies without scales. Many are covered in mucus. There are more than 800 species.

DIET

Eels often hide during the day and feed at night. Many ambush prey and attack with powerful bites. Then they swallow prey whole. Their diet includes small fish and invertebrates.

SIZE COMPARISON

2.5FT (0.76 m)

Pacific lamprey

6FT (1.8 m)

green moray eel

7FT (2.1 m)

African marbled lungfish

WHERE DO THEY LIVE?

Marine eels spend their whole lives in the ocean. Freshwater eels swim in rivers and lakes. They spawn in the ocean.

APPEARANCE

Eels have cone-shaped heads with powerful jaws. Their wide mouths contain small, sharp teeth. Long fins run along their backs to their bellies.

SPECIES PROFILE

GREEN MORAY EEL

- **Range:** tropical waters of the western Atlantic Ocean
- **Known for:** Green moray eels are actually dark gray to brown. They appear green because they are covered in thick yellow mucus. It protects the eels from parasites and diseases.

HERRING

Herring are small schooling fish. Their large schools often contain millions of fish. Herring are prey to larger fish such as salmon and tuna. They are an important food source for people too. They are often called sardines when they are canned.

WHERE DO THEY LIVE?

Herring are found in open waters near shores in the northern Atlantic and Pacific Oceans.

ATLANTIC HERRING
Range in the Wild

▼HERRING FRY

DIET

Herring are filter feeders. They mostly feed on zooplankton and fish larvae.

▲ZOOPLANKTON

SCALES▼

APPEARANCE

Herring have large, shiny scales covering their bullet-shaped bodies. Their backs are often blue. Their sides are silver.

TOGETHER AS ONE

Herring schools move as one by swimming closely together. They often form a ball shape that flattens out in shallow water.

SIZE COMPARISON

2.5FT
(0.76 m)

Pacific lamprey

1.2FT
(0.4 m)

Atlantic herring

2.2IN
(5.5 cm)

glacier lantern fish

SPECIES PROFILE

ATLANTIC HERRING

- **Range:**
  North Atlantic Ocean

- **Known for:**
  Atlantic herring are a type of forage fish. Many predator species, including marine mammals and seabirds, rely on them as a food source. They are an important part of their ecosystems.

PACIFIC SALMON

Pacific salmon are known for the migrations they make to spawn. There are seven species of Pacific salmon.

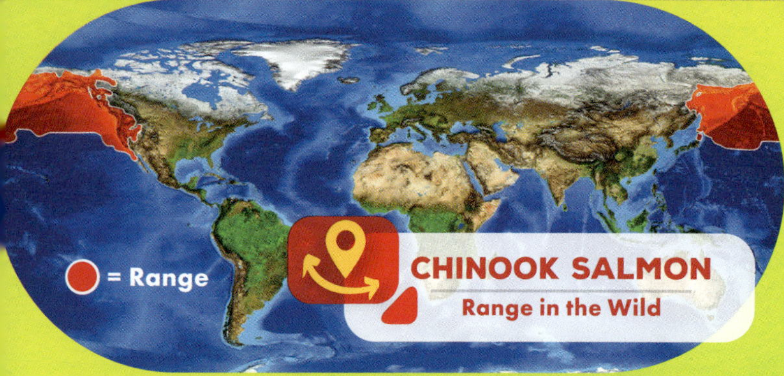

WHERE DO THEY LIVE?

Pacific salmon spend most of their lives in northern Pacific waters. They return to the freshwater streams and rivers where they hatched to spawn.

DIET

Adult salmon eat a lot to prepare for spawning. Most salmon feed on invertebrates such as squid and shrimp. They also eat small eels and other fish.

SPECIES PROFILE

CHINOOK SALMON

- **Range:**
  North Pacific Ocean

- **Known for:**
  Chinook salmon do not go through the drastic physical spawning changes that some Pacific salmon experience. Their color changes from sliver to dark bronze.

APPEARANCE

Pacific salmon are usually silver when they live in the ocean. But some species change colors in the spawning phase. Sockeye salmon develop green heads and red bodies. In most species, males grow a long, hooked upper jaw.

▼SOCKEYE SALMON

TAKE A LEAP!

Salmon are powerful swimmers. Some jump as high as 12 feet (3.7 meters).

COHO ▼SALMON

SIZE COMPARISON

1.2FT (0.4 m)

Atlantic herring

3FT (1 m)

Chinook salmon

26FT (7.9 m)

giant manta ray

LANTERN FISH

Lantern fish are small, deep-sea fish that create their own light! There are more than 240 species worldwide.

APPEARANCE

Lantern fish have large eyes and mouths. Most have dark silver bodies. Organs called photophores line their heads and undersides. These organs create blue-green light. Many species also have glowing scales along their sides.

DIET

These fish mostly eat zooplankton. They often flash their lights to draw in prey.

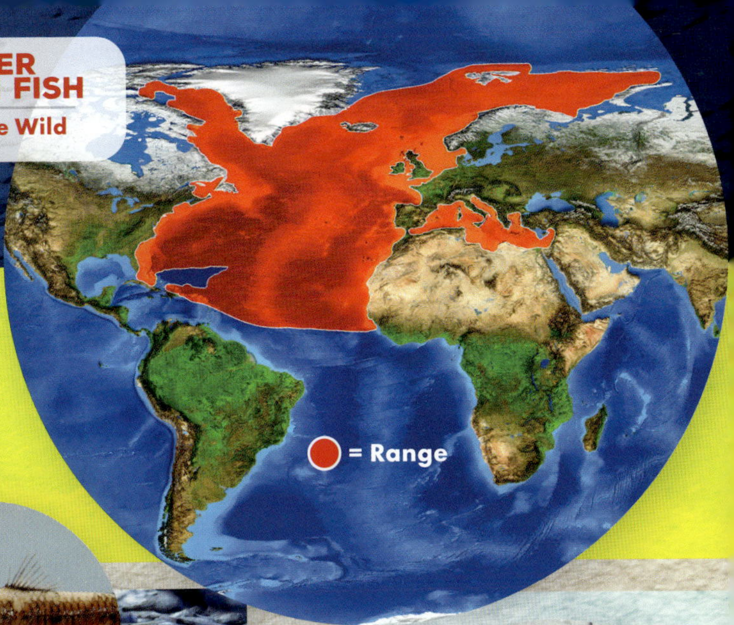

WHERE DO THEY LIVE?

Lantern fish are found in every ocean. Many species swim in deep water during the day. They go to the surface at night to feed. Some species never come to the surface.

▲ BLUNTSNOUT LANTERN FISH

HOW MANY FISH?

Around 60 percent of all deep-sea fish are lantern fish.

SIZE COMPARISON

3FT (1 m)	2.6FT (0.8 m)	2.2IN (5.5 cm)
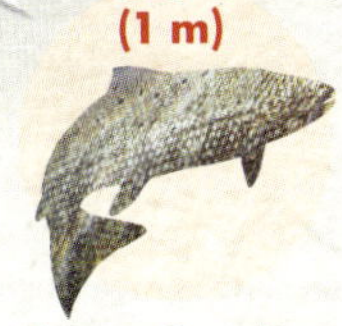		
Chinook salmon	Japanese puffer fish	glacier lantern fish

SPECIES PROFILE

GLACIER LANTERN FISH

- **Range:** North Atlantic Ocean
- **Known for:** Glacier lantern fish are one of the most common species of lantern fish in the North Atlantic Ocean. They are also one of the most studied.

CATFISH

Catfish are named for their whisker-like barbels. They are among the most common freshwater fish. There are likely more than 3,000 species.

DIET

Most catfish are scavengers that eat almost anything. They open their wide mouths to suck in small prey and plants.

APPEARANCE

The thousands of species of catfish vary in size and color. Catfish do not have scales. Some are covered in plates that are similar to armor. Others have smooth skin covered in mucus.

ELECTRIC CATFISH

Around 20 species of catfish produce electricity. They hunt prey by shocking it with a strong electric charge.

WHERE DO THEY LIVE?

Catfish are found on every continent except Antarctica. Most species live at the bottoms of lakes and rivers. A few species live in warm coastal ocean waters.

SPECIES PROFILE

MEKONG GIANT CATFISH

- **Range:** Mekong River, Southeast Asia
- **Known for:** Mekong giant catfish are the largest freshwater fish. The heaviest weigh more than 600 pounds (272 kilograms). These fish are critically endangered.

SIZE COMPARISON

2.8IN (7 cm)	6.6FT (2 m)	10FT (3 m)
lined seahorse	common monkfish	Mekong giant catfish

ANGLERFISH

Anglerfish are named for the long spines and lighted lures on their heads. The spines look like fishing poles! Only females have them. There are more than 200 species of anglerfish.

WHERE DO THEY LIVE?

Anglerfish are found in every ocean. Many swim up to 1 mile (0.6 kilometers) below the surface. Some live near the surface in tropical areas.

DIET

Female anglerfish attract prey with their spines. They snatch up invertebrates and fish that come close. Male anglerfish are parasites. They fuse with females and rely on them to survive.

SIZE COMPARISON

2.5FT (0.76 m)

Pacific lamprey

6.6FT (2 m)

common monkfish

6.6FT (2 m)

Atlantic cod

APPEARANCE

Most anglerfish are dark gray to dark brown. Sharp teeth fill their large, downward-pointing mouths.

SPECIES PROFILE

COMMON MONKFISH

- **Range:** northern Atlantic Ocean and Mediterranean Sea

- **Known for:** Monkfish are a common sight at food markets, especially in parts of Europe. Their tail meat tastes similar to lobster.

COD

Cod are important to ocean food chains. They are prey to many larger fish and sea mammals. Many people also eat cod. There are four species.

APPEARANCE

Cod have large heads and heavy bodies. Three fins line their backs. These fish can be gray, green, or reddish-brown. Some are spotted.

PACIFIC COD ▲

SPECIES PROFILE

ATLANTIC COD

- **Range:** North Atlantic Ocean
- **Known for:** Atlantic cod fishing was one of the first major businesses in colonial America. But hundreds of years of overfishing has harmed the species. Today, their populations are vulnerable.

ALASKA POLLOCK ▼

▲ATLANTIC COD

DIET

Cod usually feed at dawn and dusk. Their barbels sense fish and invertebrates along the seafloor. They are also known to eat squid.

SIZE COMPARISON

2.5FT (0.76 m)	6.5FT (2 m)	6.6FT (2 m)
Pacific lamprey	Atlantic bluefin tuna	Atlantic cod

WHERE DO THEY LIVE?

Cod are found in the Atlantic, Pacific, and Arctic Oceans. Many cod are bottom dwellers. They may be found in coastal waters or the deep sea.

ATLANTIC COD
Range in the Wild

GREENLAND
▼COD

SEAHORSES

Seahorses get their name from their heads. They are similar in shape to horse heads. Seahorses swim slowly with their bodies upright. There are around 50 species of seahorses.

PYGMY ▲ SEAHORSE

LINED SEAHORSE
Range in the Wild

WHERE DO THEY LIVE?

Seahorses live in tropical and temperate coastal waters. They are often found in coral reefs, mangroves, and seagrass beds. Some swim in estuaries.

DIET

Seahorses are ambush predators. They suck zooplankton and other tiny animals into their mouths.

THORNY ▼ SEAHORSE

SIZE COMPARISON

2.8IN (7 cm)	2.6FT (0.8 m)	2.5FT (0.76 m)
lined seahorse	Japanese puffer fish	Pacific lamprey

SPECIES PROFILE

LINED SEAHORSE

- **Range:** western Atlantic Ocean
- **Known for:** Lined seahorses are named for their pattern of white lines. This species is vulnerable due to habitat loss, capture for aquariums, and bycatch.

SEEING ALL AROUND

Seahorse eyes can look in two different directions. These fish can see in front of and behind themselves at the same time.

APPEARANCE

Seahorses' horselike heads end with toothless, tube-shaped snouts. Fins on the sides of their heads help them steer as they swim. Their long bodies are covered in rings of bony plates. These fish grab hold of plants with their forward-curling tails.

TUNA

Tuna are some of the fastest fish on Earth. They can swim more than 40 miles (64 kilometers) per hour. There are seven species of tuna.

BLACKFIN ▲ TUNA

SCHOOL OF ▼ TUNA

DIET

Tuna eat whatever they can catch. They use super speeds to ambush prey. Common meals include small fish, squid, and shellfish.

YELLOWFIN ▼ TUNA

SPECIES PROFILE

ATLANTIC BLUEFIN TUNA

Range:
Atlantic Ocean

Known for:
Atlantic bluefin tuna are among the largest and fastest fish in the world. They are popular among sport fishers. The largest recorded catch weighed 1,496 pounds (679 kilograms)!

ATLANTIC BLUEFIN TUNA

Range in the Wild

WHERE DO THEY LIVE?

Tuna are found in temperate and tropical oceans. They prefer open waters near the surface. Many make long migrations from one ocean to another.

APPEARANCE

Most tuna have dark backs and shiny, silver bellies. They have torpedo-shaped bodies and large, forked tails. Small ridges stick out along the base of their tails.

SIZE COMPARISON

3FT (1 m)

Chinook salmon

6.5FT (2 m)

Atlantic bluefin tuna

26FT (8 m)

beluga sturgeon

PUFFER FISH

Puffer fish can take in water to puff up their bodies like a ball. They inflate so suddenly that they often scare predators away. There are more than 120 species of puffers.

APPEARANCE

Puffers have large heads and long, scaleless bodies. Their coloring varies greatly by species. Some puffers are covered in sharp spines. Most have rough skin.

▲ SPOTTED SHARPNOSE PUFFER

◀ YELLOW NORTHERN PUFFER

DIET

Puffers have sharp, beak-like teeth that they may use to crush the hard shells of crustaceans. Most puffer fish eat invertebrates and algae.

WHITE-SPOTTED ▶ PUFFER

TOXIC FISH

Most puffer fish carry a highly toxic poison in some of their organs.

WHERE DO THEY LIVE?

Puffers are found in warm oceans. They often live around coral reefs and seagrass beds. Some species live in fresh water.

PEA PUFFER FISH▼ in fresh water

MAP PUFFER▲

SIZE COMPARISON

SPECIES PROFILE

JAPANESE PUFFER FISH

- **Range:** northwest Pacific Ocean, Sea of Japan, East China Sea, Yellow Sea
- **Known for:** Japanese puffers are also known as tiger puffers. Their meat is a delicacy in Japan called *fugu*. Only expertly trained chefs can prepare fugu. The meat can be deadly if it is not prepared correctly!

FISH AND PEOPLE

People have depended on fish for thousands of years. Fish are eaten by billions of people worldwide. Fishing gives millions of workers jobs. It is also a popular pastime and sport. Scuba divers enjoy swimming with fish in nature. Many people keep fish as pets.

AQUARIUM FISH

FISH FARMING

Fish adapt well to living in captivity. This allows scientists to study their behaviors, bodies, and presence in habitats. Fish also help control diseases outside the lab. Many eat the larvae of mosquitoes that can spread diseases.

FOLKLORE PROFILE

NAME:

KOI FISH

COUNTRY:

CHINA

FAMOUS FOR:

Chinese legend states that a group of koi once traveled up the Yellow River. They tried to swim up an enormous waterfall. Those that reached the top were turned into powerful dragons. They symbolize strength, perseverance, and transformation.

Fish help humans in many ways. But human behaviors are not always kind to fish. Overfishing has lowered fish numbers in many places. Construction has destroyed habitats and spawning grounds. Pollution changes and harms fish habitats.

POLLUTION

OVERFISHING

FISH SANCTUARY

Many people work to protect fish. Governments set yearly catch limits for fishers. They also create areas where fishing is banned. Some organizations clean up places harmed by waste and garbage. Others work to restore habitats. People must work together to keep fish safe!

GLOSSARY

adapted—changed over a period of time

ambush—to attack from a hiding place

barbels—whisker-like body parts around the mouths of some fish that are used to find food

bioluminescence—the ability of a living thing to produce light due to a chemical reaction in the body

cartilage—stretchy tissue that makes up parts of an animal's body

countershading—a type of coloring in which the top of the body is darker than the lower parts of the body; countershading is a type of camouflage.

diverse—made up of animals that are different from one another

estuaries—water passages where ocean tides and river currents meet

evolved—changed from one form into a new form

fertilize—to make a plant or animal able to produce life; fertilization occurs when a male's sperm joins with a female's egg to create young.

filter feeders—animals that get food by filtering water currents to obtain tiny plants and animals

habitats—natural homes of plants and animals

hemisphere—a half of the earth

larvae—young

mammals—warm-blooded animals that have backbones and feed their young milk

mangroves—groups of trees and shrubs that grow along coastlines

migrate—to move from one place to another

parasites—living things that use other living things to survive; parasites often harm their hosts.

pectoral fins—a pair of fins on the side of a fish that control a fish's movement

pollution—substances that make the earth dirty or unsafe; pollution usually comes from humans' actions.

scavengers—animals that feed on the rotting meat of a dead animal

snouts—the noses and mouths of some animals

spawn—to produce young by releasing eggs

species—groups of living things that are alike and can reproduce with one another

temperate—having a moderate climate with no temperature extremes

tropical—related to the tropics; the tropics is a hot, rainy region near the equator.

vertebrates—animals with backbones; invertebrates are animals without backbones.

WRITE ABOUT IT!

- What species of fish would you like to learn more about? **Why?**
- What fish adaptation do you think is the most interesting? **Why?**
- **What** changes can you make in your life that could help keep fish habitats safe?

ALSO CHECK OUT

INDEX

anglerfish, 12, 32–33
catfish, 8, 12, 30–31
cod, 34–35
eels, 12, 22–23, 26
evolutionary excellence, 7
herring, 9, 24–25
koi fish, 43
lampreys, 13, 14–15
lantern fish, 28–29
lungfish, 12, 18–19
Pacific salmon, 9, 26–27
puffer fish, 12, 40–41
rays, 9, 13, 16–17
seahorses, 12, 36–37
species profile, 15, 19, 21, 23, 25, 27, 29, 31, 33, 34, 37, 38, 41
sturgeons, 9, 12, 20–21
taxonomy chart, 5
tuna, 12, 24, 38–39
vulnerable species, 17

The images in this book are reproduced through the courtesy of: yeshaya, front cover, p. 37; mathefoto, front cover; Bekheet, front cover; PNGLovers, front cover; Ophelia, front cover; satit, front cover; crisod, pp. 3, 10; 016Graphics, p. 3; Martin Prochazkacz, p. 4 (marlin); Heiko Jetzkowitz, p. 4 (flounders); Heidi's Pics, p. 4 (sea dragon); Sergiu, p. 4 (betta); Roman, p. 5 (koi); titipong8176734, p. 5 (cichlid); Eric Isselée, pp. 5 (cowfish), 18-19 (main); Stocktrek Images, Inc./ Alamy, p. 6 (jawless); Danny Ye, p. 6 (model); National Science Foundation Multimedia Gallery/ Wikimedia Commons, p. 6 (fun fact); besjunior, p. 6 (catfish); Daniel Thornberg, pp. 7 (top), 26-27 (main); taitai6769, p. 7 (left); dmf87, p. 7 (right); Nature Picture Library/ Alamy, pp. 8 (seahorse), 15 (profile); SergeUWPhoto, pp. 8 (jawfish), 11 (right); ZCOOL HelloRF, p. 8 (eggs); Przemek Iciak, p. 8 (angelfish); Studio 37, p. 9 (top); Mediterranean/ Getty Images, p. 9 (herring); Endless luck, p. 9 (sturgeon); StayAhead, p. 9 (ray); USFWS Fish and Aquatic Conservation/ Wikimedia Commons, p. 9 (salmon); Neil Bromhall, p. 10 (anglerfish); whitcomberd, pp. 10 (school), 33 (bottom); Andrea Izzotti, pp. 11 (top), 18 (bottom); ACHPF, p. 11 (middle); Brandon Olafasson, p. 11 (bottom); Ken Griffiths, p. 12 (lungfish); scaliger, p. 12 (sturgeon); zilvergolf, p. 12 (seahorse); Subphoto, p. 12 (catfish); Jonathan, p. 12 (tuna); Miroslav Halama, pp. 12 (puffer), 40 (bottom); Wirestock Creators, p. 13 (ray); jack perks, p. 13 (lamprey); Gena Melendrez, p. 14 (teeth); Great Lakes Fishery Commission/ Wikimedia Commons, p. 14; Valerii Evlakhov, pp. 14-15 (main), 22-23 (main); Ari, p. 16 (main); Simon Fraser University/ Wikimedia Commons, p. 16 (sawfish); aquapix, p. 16; Max Frey, p. 16 (stingray); Inna, p. 17 (fun fact, left); Aaron, p. 17 (right); Animal Stock/ Alamy, p. 18 (top); Fab, p. 18 (left); paparazzza, p. 18 (Australian); Vassil/ Wikimedia Commons, p. 19; eathercollector, p. 19 (profile); Karel Bartik, p. 20 (top, right); prochym, p. 20 (middle); Martin Rejzek, p. 20 (left); Rostislav Stefanek, p. 21 (profile); FomaA, p. 21 (fun fact); etiana, pp. 20-21 (main); JackF, p. 21 (right); Renar, p. 22 (wolf); Ethan Daniels, p. 22 (ribbon); RLS Photo, p. 22 (fresh); estionx, p. 22; Sergey p. 23; Wet Lizard, p. 23 (profile); Jon Anders Wiken, p. 24; Radovan, p. 24 (main); Flowworks.one, p. 24; Olivier Dugornay/ Wikimedia Commons, p. 24 (fry); Leonardo Gonzalez, p. 25 (top, fun fact); Choksawatdikorn, p. 25 (zooplankton); OMD, p. 25 (scales); Bob Pool, p. 25; Mediterranean, p. 25 (profile); divedog, p. 26 (top); Paul, p. 26 (spawning); Sekar B, p. 26; Conrad, p. 26 (chum); CSNafzger, p. 27 (profile, sockeye); Bureau of Land Management Oregon and Washington/ Wikimedia Commons, p. 27 (coho); Shorif creative, pp. 28-29 (main); Cavan, p. 28; 3dsam79, p. 28 (left); Morgan Trimble/ Alamy, p. 28 (right); SEFSC Pascagoula Laboratory/ Wikimedia Commons, p. 29 (bluntsnout); Cavan Images/ Alamy, p. 29; HulloThere/ Wikimedia Commons, p. 29 (profile); Rostislav, p. 30 (wels); kichigin19, p. 30 (striped); Juancajuarez, p. 30 (sucker); Egor Chernyakov/Wirestock, p. 30 (tiger); S Widodo, p. 30; Sophia, pp. 30-31 (main); Alexander Iwan, p. 31; Bill, p. 31 (profile); Janik Rybicka, p. 32 (top); Raimundo Fernandez Diez/ Getty Images, p. 32 (middle); Tommi Kokkola Photography/ Getty Images, p. 32 (bottom); zcw, p. 33 (main); GeraldRobertFischer, p. 33; valda butterworth, p. 33 (profile); dule964, pp. 34-35 (main); Andy Murch/ Ocean Wide Images, p. 34 (top); mirecca, p. 34 (profile); DoublePhoto studio, p. 34 (bottom); Elena, p. 35 (top); RLS Photo/ Alamy, p. 35; Ed Brown, p. 36 (top); The Ocean Agency, p. 36 (left); Richard Whitcombe, p. 36 (right); Brent, p. 37 (profile); Julia, p. 37 (main); DP0305, p. 37 (bottom); ftlaudgirl, p. 38 (top); Guido, p. 38 (school); Jemma Craig, p. 38; nicolas, p. 38 (yellowfin); patileac, p. 38 (profile); Andrei, p. 39 (main); Rob, p. 39; Florin, p. 40 (main); Nick Hobgood/ Wikimedia Commons, p. 40 (top); Hafit Irawan, p. 40 (middle); Keat Eung, p. 41 (map); Chonlasub, p. 41 (pea); Jye Shen, p. 41 (profile); Dmytro Sheremeta, p. 42 (top); coffmancmu, p. 42 (middle); Leonid, p. 42 (bottom); Miguel, p. 43 (larvae); Xinhua News Agency/ Getty Images, p. 43; Maria, p. 43 (koi); Dina, p. 43 (profile); Guosheng Wu, p. 43 (river); somchairakin, p. 44 (top); Azim Aunon, p. 44 (middle); Michael Dechev, p. 44 (left); Siam, p. 44 (right); Mohamad alias, p. 45 (top); Adriana Iacob, p. 45 (middle); Marigold, p. 45 (left); Magic Orb Studio, p. 45 (right).